Clever Crafts

Fun with NATURE

Annalees Lim

WINDMILL BOOKS

New York

Published in 2013 by Windmill Books, An Imprint of Rosen Publishing
29 East 21st Street, New York, NY 10010

Editor for Wayland: Victoria Brooker
US Editor: Sara Antill
Designer: Lisa Peacock
Photographer: Simon Pask
US Book Layout: Greg Tucker

Library of Congress Cataloging-in-Publication Data

Lim, Annalees.
 Fun with nature / by Annalees Lim.
    p. cm. — (Clever crafts)
 Includes index.
 ISBN 978-1-4777-0181-2 (library binding) — ISBN 978-1-4777-0190-4 (pbk.) —
 ISBN 978-1-4777-0191-1 (6-pack)
 1. Nature craft—Juvenile literature. I. Title.
 TT157.L449 2013
 745.58'4—dc23

2012026228

Manufactured in the United States of America

CPSIA Compliance Information: Batch #BW13WM: For Further Information contact Windmill Books, New York, New York at 1-866-478-0556

Contents

Fun with Nature

You can have lots of fun with nature! You just have to step outside and look around you! Collect stones, shells, twigs, and leaves when you're out and about to make fantastic pieces of art.

Be inspired by the natural world that you pass by every day. Notice the trees changing through the seasons from young, green shoots emerging in spring to the red and brown leaves falling in autumn. Every season there are new materials for you to use!

Always ask a grown up before you pick anything up. Lots of things should stay where you find them. A good rule is to only collect what has fallen from plants or trees and never pick anything that is still alive or growing. Remember to wash your findings before you use them.

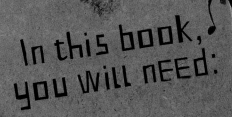

In this book, you will need:

Paint and paintbrushes

To decorate your crafts. Use poster paints or acrylic paints.

Paper or cardboard

To display or decorate your crafts.

Clay

Air-drying clay can be found in most craft stores and even in some larger supermarkets.

Glue

Use strong glue that will stick different materials together. If you are gluing any fabric remember to use fabric glue.

Scissors

Use child-size scissors. Ask an adult to help where suggested, or with any tricky parts.

Mini-Greenhouse Planter

You will need:
One 2-liter drink bottle
Scissors
Electrical tape or masking tape
Plastic food tray or plant pot base
Green construction paper
Tape
Soil
Seeds

Nurture small seeds into little plants before you plant them outside with this indoor greenhouse! All you need is a plastic bottle, a base, some soil, and some seeds!

1

Ask an adult to cut the bottle in half. You will only need the top half for this project. Put masking tape around the cut edge to make it less sharp.

2

Using the tape, create the lines of your greenhouse, starting with the walls and roof.

There is no need to throw away the leftover plastic bottle. Try covering it in papier-mâché, leaving it to dry and then painting it to create a handy pencil holder!

3

Make windows and a door with the tape.

4

Cut some green construction paper into the shape of grass. Stick this green paper to the plastic tray.

5

Fill the tray with soil and plant your seeds. Cover the seeds with the plastic greenhouse and leave to grow, watering occasionally.

Leafy Print Wrapping Paper

You will need:
Leaves
Large piece of paper
Paint
Paintbrush

Create your own unique wrapping paper all year-round by using leaves you have collected from the garden or a walk in the park.

1

Choose a selection of leaves that are different shapes and sizes.

2

Paint a thin layer of paint onto one of the leaves. Remember to do this on top of a scrap piece of paper so you don't make a mess!

3

Place the painted side of your leaf onto your large piece of paper and press down lightly to create a print.

4

Repeat with different colors and leaf shapes until the whole piece of paper is covered. Leave to dry before you wrap your present!

Make your wrapping paper extra special by adding some glitter glue to the outside of the leaves to make them sparkle. You can even try printing onto colored paper!

Seashell Clay Prints

You will need:
- Cardboard
- Butter knife
- Air-drying clay
- Rolling pin
- A collection of seashells
- Paint
- Paintbrush
- Pencil
- Yarn or string

Make use of any seashells you find on vacation by creating a decorative clay print. It is perfect to hang in your room and remind you of lovely times you had at the seaside!

1

Roll out the air-drying clay until it is about 1 inch (2.5 cm) thick.

2

Using a cardboard template that is about 4 inches by 4 inches (10 cm x 10 cm), cut a square shape out of the clay using an old butter knife.

3

Choose your favorite seashells and gently press them into the soft clay to make prints.

4

Use the handle of a paintbrush to make two holes at the top of the tile. Leave to dry in a dry warm place for about 1-2 days.

5

Once the whole tile is completely dry, decorate using acrylic paints. Leave to dry and thread some yarn through the holes to hang it up!

11

Pinecone Hedgehog Family

Make your own hedgehog family using pinecones that you can find on a woodland walk!

You will need:

Pinecones
Beige, white, and blue clay
Paintbrush
Sharp pencil

1

Using some beige colored clay, mold a cone shape for the face, two flat disks for ears, and four small balls for the feet.

Pinecones are not the only natural craft material you can find in the woods. Make crazy chestnut creatures or adorable acorn animals using the same techniques.

2

Press the clay cone onto the front of the pinecone until it is stuck firmly in place. Next press the ears on top. Use the handle of a paintbrush to make a dip in each ear.

3

Use the handle of the paintbrush again to create two holes for the eyes. Carefully use a sharp pencil to create a slit for the mouth.

4

Turn the hedgehog over and press the four balls onto the bottom of the pinecone to make the feet.

5

Mold two white and two blue balls for the eyes. Fill the holes you made in the cone-shape face with these balls. Your first family member is ready! Now you can make more!

Dried Flower Field

You will need:
Flowers
Paper
Heavy books
Construction paper in blue,
  green, yellow, and white
Green tissue paper
Scissors
Glue

Make pretty flowers last forever by drying them out and creating a beautiful picture of a field in bloom.

1

Place a selection of flowers between two sheets of paper and place the paper between two heavy books. Leave for 2-4 weeks to dry out.

2

In the meantime, cut some clouds out of white paper and a wavy shape out of green paper to make rolling hills.

3

Cut out a circle from some yellow paper and some long triangles to make the Sun's rays.

You could use your dried flowers for many craft projects. Make a picture of a vase of flowers or glue them onto a box to make a lovely birthday gift.

4

Cut out some stems and leaves for the flowers from the green tissue paper.

5

Glue all of the paper pieces onto the blue construction paper. Then glue the dried flowers onto the green stems. Your picture is complete!

Mini Forest

You will need:
Twigs
String
Plastic yogurt container
Stones or pebbles
Green tissue paper
Glue
Scissors

Create your very own
enchanted forest inside
a house from sticks
you've collected from
your garden, a park, or
a walk in the woods.

Who could live in your forest? Maybe
you could draw and cut out people
to wander through the trees or use it as a
home for the hedgehog family you can
make on pages 12-13.

1

Bundle together some twigs. Tie the bundle together with some string.

2

Place the twigs in the yogurt container and fill it with the small stones so that the miniature tree can stand on its own.

3

Cut out small leaf shapes from the tissue paper. You can decide whether you want spring green trees, red and orange trees for autumn, or a multicolored magical forest using blues and purple.

4

Glue the leaves onto the ends of the twigs to make full branches. Now make some more to fill your forest.

Stone Painting

You will need:
Stones, pebbles, and rocks
Paint
Paintbrush
Glue
Googly eyes
White felt
Scissors

Create many colorful creatures by painting rocks, pebbles, or stones. These buzzing bees make great ornaments, colorful bookends, or pretty paper weights.

Your stone collection can be made into any animal you want. Just think about what shape stones will be best to use and what colors you'll need.

Choose a stone and paint it yellow. Leave to dry in a warm place.

Once the yellow paint is dry, paint three thick black stripes onto the stone.

Use glue to stick two googly eyes onto the front of the stone.

Cut out some wings from the white felt. Glue to the top of the stone and leave to dry completely.

Nature Family Portraits

You will need:

Leaves
Colored and white paper
Magazines
Scissors
Glue
Black felt-tip pen

Create crazy family portraits by using leaves and other craft materials.

If you want your family portraits to look exactly like the members of your family, take photographs and print them out. You can then cut out people's features and stick them onto the leafy heads and bodies.

1

Glue a leaf onto a colored piece of paper. This will make the head of your portrait.

2

Cut out eyes, noses, mouths, ears, and hair from different people in an old magazine. Choose some and glue in place on the leaf.

3

Once the glue is dry, cut out the head, leaving a small border of colored paper.

4

Glue this onto the white paper. Draw some arms and legs to create your person. Make lots of people and glue them onto the same page to make a family!

Nature Crown

You will need:

Twigs
Glue
Paintbrush
Leaves
Tissue paper
Thick gold paper
Stapler
Sheet of plastic

If you have made too many leaves or twig triangles, try gluing them onto lengths of string to make a cool hanging for your window.

Be the king or queen of the forest with this spectacular nature crown.

1 Cut the tissue paper into rectangles. Paint with glue. Lay three twigs on top in a triangle shape. Fold the tissue paper over the twigs and paint on more glue. Make about 6 triangles and leave to dry.

2 On a sheet of plastic, cover a sheet of tissue paper in glue. The plastic makes the tissue paper easier to peel off when dry. Stick some leaves onto the sheet. Make two of these sheets in different colors.

3

Once the sheets are dry, cut the leaves out keeping a colored border around the leaves.

4

Staple strips of gold paper together to make a crown that will fit onto your head.

5

Use tape or glue to attach the triangles and leaves to complete your crown.

Glossary

greenhouse (GREEN-hows) A building used to grow plants all year long. It usually has a glass roof and glass walls.

nurture (NUR-chur) To encourage the growth of plants by watching and watering them when necessary.

paper weight (PAY-per WAYT) A small heavy object placed on top of papers to stop them from moving in the wind or by accident.

shoots (SHOOTZ) A new growth on a tree or plant.

technique (tek-NEEK) A particular way of doing something.

template (TEM-plut) A shape used as a guide for drawing or cutting.

unique (yoo-NEEK) Different from everything else.

Index

Websites

For web resources related to the subject of this book, go to: www.windmillbooks.com/weblinks and select this book's title.

24